Other Badger Biographies

BASEBALL HERO

BOB KANN

WISCONSIN HISTORICAL SOCIETY PRESS

Published by the Wisconsin Historical Society Press
Publishers since 1855

©2012 by the State Historical Society of Wisconsin

Publication of this book was made possible in part by a grant from the D.C. Everest fellowship fund.

wisconsin**history**.org

Photographs identified with WHi are from the Society's collections; address requests to reproduce these photos to the Visual Materials Archivist at the Wisconsin Historical Society, 816 State Street, Madison, WI 53706.

Printed in Wisconsin, U.S.A.
Designed by Jill Bremigan

16 15 14 13 12   1 2 3 4 5

Library of Congress Cataloging-in-Publication Data
Kann, Bob.
 Joyce Westerman : baseball hero / Bob Kann.
    p. cm. — (Badger biographies)
 Includes bibliographical references and index.
 ISBN 978-0-87020-486-9 (pbk. : alk. paper) 1. Westerman, Joyce. 2. Women baseball players—United States—Biography. 3. Women baseball players—Wisconsin—Biography. 4. All-American Girls Professional Baseball League—History. I. Title.
 GV865.W444K36 2012
 796.357092—dc23
 [B]
                          2011021459

∞ The paper used in this publication meets the minimum requirements of the American National Standard for Information Sciences—Permanence of Paper for Printed Library Materials, ANSI Z39.48-1992.

For Caroline and Shayle

Contents

1

Sometimes Dreams Come True

When Joyce Hill was 5 years old, her uncle threw a ball to her. Joyce caught the ball and threw it back to him. This was the first time she had played "catch." Joyce loved it. She began to play ball whenever she could. Before long, she dreamed of becoming a **professional** baseball player. When Joyce was a little girl, there was no professional baseball **league** for women. But that didn't stop Joyce from dreaming.

Fourteen years later, her dream came true. Joyce became one of more than 550 women who played in the All-American Girls Professional Baseball League from 1943 to 1954. As a professional player, Joyce was paid to play baseball in this league. But she would have played for free because it was so much fun!

professional (pruh **fesh** uh nul): someone who is paid to do something   **league** (leeg): an organized group of sports clubs or teams

For 8 of the league's 12 years, Joyce traveled around the United States playing ball. She played catcher, right field, and first base.

In 1988, Joyce and the other women from the league received the highest **award** baseball players can receive. They were honored in the National Baseball Hall of Fame in a new **exhibit** called *Women in Baseball*. Four years after that, Joyce and the other players became famous because of a movie about women's baseball called *A League of Their Own*. This book tells the story of how a farm girl from Wisconsin made her dreams come true.

award: an honor or present given to someone for doing something special   **exhibit** (eg **zib** it): a public display of interesting things, often at a museum

2

Losing Their Home

Joyce Hill was born in Kenosha, Wisconsin, on December 29, 1925. Nobody imagined that she would grow up to help change the idea that women couldn't play baseball. But that's just what she did.

Joyce's parents, **Cecil** Hill and Lillian Clausen Hill, were born in Wisconsin. Their parents came to Wisconsin from Denmark, Sweden, and Germany. Joyce had 3 older sisters and 4 younger brothers.

COURTESY OF JOYCE WESTERMAN

The Hill family in the 1920s. Young Joyce is sitting on the arm of the chair behind her baby brother.

Cecil: see suhl

When Joyce was 5 years old, she used to play catch with her Uncle Lon. Sometimes he threw the ball so hard it bent her thumb back. Even though it hurt, she loved playing ball.

Joyce attended first grade at Roosevelt Elementary School in Kenosha. She walked to school every day. She often played **marbles** before school.

Joyce liked marbles, but not as much as she liked playing ball.

But at recess, Joyce liked to play softball with the boys. In those days, it was unusual for girls to play softball or baseball. And if girls did play, they didn't play with boys. But Joyce played with boys—and she could hit the ball better than they could! Instead of feeling proud, Joyce felt **embarrassed** because girls weren't supposed to be better players than boys.

marbles: a children's game in which colorful glass balls are rolled along on the ground   **embarrassed**: feeling shy or uneasy about something

In 1931, when Joyce was 5 years old, her family lost their home. Like many other people during the **Great Depression**, Joyce's father could not earn enough money to pay the **mortgage** on his family's home. Before, he had worked in a

factory making cars for the Nash **Motors** Company. But during the Great Depression, few people had enough money to buy cars. So workers at

A car being made at the Nash Motors Company

Nash Motors were **laid off** from their jobs.

With Joyce's father no longer working, the rest of the Hill family tried to earn money any way they could. Joyce's mother began to bake bread and rolls. Joyce and her sisters sold the baked goods in their neighborhood.

Great Depression: the decade of the 1930s when many people in the United States had no jobs and were very poor **mortgage** (**mor** gij): money lent by a bank to buy a house **motor**: engine **laid off**: sent home from a job without pay because there is not enough work to do

Soon the Hill family could no longer afford to live in their home. They moved into an old house owned by Joyce's grandfather and uncle in Pleasant Prairie, Wisconsin. The house was so old that one part was falling down and couldn't be used. Joyce's family lived in the rest of the house. Unlike their home in Kenosha, this house had no electricity or running water. It was heated with a **potbellied stove**. They had to burn coal or wood in the stove to heat the house.

The Great Depression

For many people, the 1920s were a good time. There were good factory jobs making farm **equipment**, cars, and other goods. And American farmers had increased their crops because of **World War I**. Their crops fed soldiers and people in Europe, where many farms were destroyed.

Almost everyone believed that the country's **economy** was getting better and better. Many people borrowed money from banks to buy cars, homes, and other goods. But the banks lent too much money. Prices fell. Banks failed. Factories closed. People lost their jobs.

potbellied stove: a round iron stove that burns wood or coal and looks like a big belly
equipment (ee **kwip** muhnt): tools and machines needed or used for a particular purpose
World War I: conflict between the Allied Powers (France, Great Britain, Russia, and the United States) and the Central Powers (Germany, the Ottoman Empire, and Austria-Hungary) that lasted from 1914 to 1918
economy (ee **kahn** uh mee): the amount of goods, services, and money that are made, bought, and sold by a group of people

6

A Wisconsin family during the Great Depression. Can you see their potbellied stove?

The Great Depression began in 1929. Between 1930 and 1933, nearly half of the factory workers in Wisconsin lost their jobs, just like Joyce's father did. Many families lost their homes.

People all over the country suffered. Men, women, and children known as **hoboes** traveled on railroad boxcars looking for work. More than 250,000 teenage hoboes wandered across America during the Great Depression. Boys and girls as young as 12 years old left home because there was no food to eat.

In a way, Joyce and her family were lucky during the Great Depression. Although they lost their home, they were able to move to a farm. They always had a roof over their heads. They had plenty of food, the family stayed together, and the children had happy childhoods.

Hoboes

hobo (hoh boh): a person who is poor and homeless, and often rides trains looking for work

The Hills' new home was near railroad tracks. Sometimes coal would fall off trains as they passed. Joyce, her brothers and sisters, and her mother would collect the coal and bring it back home to heat the stove. This coal was free, and the family had to save money any way they could.

Joyce's mother usually was very quiet. To Joyce, she seemed too busy working to talk. Like Joyce's father, she worked very hard, especially during the Depression. But Joyce never heard her parents complain. She learned to work hard from her parents. Her father used to say, "You give a person 8 hours of work for 8 hours of pay. You do your very best. You don't just put in your time."

Joyce and her brothers and sisters were happy to live in Pleasant Prairie, even without running water or electricity in their home. Her uncle and grandfather owned more than 100 **acres** of land. The kids explored the woods and played on the farm. There was a pond nearby where they skated in the winter. They had few toys, but they were happy playing together.

acre (**ay** kur): a measurement of area that is almost the size of a football field

Joyce's new school in Pleasant Prairie was called Star School. There was only one teacher for all 8 grades. It was just down the road from Joyce's new home. Her mother had also attended Star School. Joyce even had the same teacher at Star School that her mother had.

Just like at her old school, Joyce loved to play ball during recess. She mostly played with boys, but a few girls would play too. Joyce was usually the captain of her team because she was one of the best players.

Joyce remembers one game when she was the pitcher. The batter hit a **line drive**, and the ball hit Joyce in the throat. Years later, she still remembers that it hurt a lot. But Joyce loved baseball, so she continued to play.

WHI IMAGE ID 6739

Playing ball at recess

line drive: a baseball hit fast and close to the ground rather than high in the air

3

"Wow, She Can Really Work"

Joyce was her father's favorite helper. Whatever he did, Joyce wanted to do too.

When Joyce was 8 years old, she helped her father cut down trees. Joyce would work one end of a 2-person saw, and her father would be on the other end. Together they'd saw down trees, use the wood for their stove, and heat their home.

When Joyce was 10 years old, she started her first paying job. During the summer, she and her brothers and sisters worked on their neighbor's farm. They pulled weeds for 10 cents an hour. They also picked strawberries and tomatoes. They were paid by how much they picked.

The Hill children might work as long as 8 hours a day. It was tiring working on their hands and knees all day, but it was a way to help their family. They used the money they earned to buy school clothes. With many children in the family to feed, everyone had to help out.

Picking vegetables is hard work.

Joyce was able to save some of the money she earned. When she was 11 years old, she very badly wanted to own a bicycle. None of her brothers or sisters owned a bicycle, but she had learned how to ride on her cousin's bike. After she had saved $5, her uncle took her to Kenosha. He knew someone selling a girl's bicycle. Joyce bought the bike and happily rode it for many years.

COURTESY OF JOYCE WESTERMAN

Joyce with her bicycle

When Joyce was 13 years old, she'd wake up at 5 o'clock in the morning. She hurried to the barn to finish her uncle's farm chores before he even came outside. It was a matter of pride for her. Whatever job Joyce did, she tried to do her very best. If she had to sweep the floors after the cows went out to the pasture, she'd make sure the barn floors were swept completely clean and covered with **lime**. When Joyce finished doing chores for her uncle, she felt wonderful. She said, "Walking out the barn, I'd feel like I was 10 feet tall. It was the greatest feeling to do that."

Joyce did many jobs that her sisters and younger brothers wouldn't do. When she was 14 years old, Joyce would drive her uncle's truck out to the field to feed cornstalks to the

lime: a white powder used to keep barn floors dry and clean

steers. She did this even though she was too young to drive **legally**. When Joyce was a little older, she drove a tractor and plowed the fields.

Sometimes Joyce worked in her uncle's fields with other men.

A young woman like Joyce driving a tractor

She usually wore jeans and tucked her short hair under a cap. The men would ask, "Is that a girl or a boy?" Joyce's uncle would answer that she was a girl. The men would say, "Wow, she can really work."

Joyce also helped her uncle unload heavy sacks of grain from trucks. Joyce's aunt thought this was terrible. She believed only men should do heavy lifting. She told Joyce, "You are never going to amount to anything. . . . You'll never get married and never be a good **homemaker**."

steer: a young male cow raised especially for its beef   **legally**: in a way that is allowed by law
homemaker: the member of a family who takes care of the home and children

13

When Joyce heard this, she thought, "I'll show her." Many years later she did. She got married and was an excellent homemaker. She could cook and bake good food just as well as her mom.

Some people called Joyce a tomboy. This meant that she did many things that boys usually did. But Joyce loved helping her dad and her uncle so much that she didn't care what other people said.

Joyce also participated in **4-H** from the time she was 9 years old until she finished high school. She really liked working with cattle. Her uncle gave her a calf to

Joyce with one of her calves

4-H: a club where kids learn about farming, healthy living, science, and other life skills

14

take care of. She brushed it, cleaned it, and made sure it was standing straight. She showed the calf at the county fair and won several ribbons. She even trained one calf to follow her around.

During the Depression, Joyce's father raised chickens and turkeys. Before Thanksgiving each year, Joyce took a few days off from school to help her father get the turkeys ready to sell. Joyce's teachers didn't like that she missed school, but Joyce's father needed her help. Joyce didn't mind missing school. She said, "You just did what you had to do."

Joyce would **dress** the turkeys and pull out their **pinfeathers**. She used **pliers** to pull out the small feathers that stayed stuck in the turkey. Joyce also did this same job at other farms to carn money.

Throughout Joyce's childhood, she liked to listen to Chicago Cubs baseball games on the radio. One of her biggest **thrills** was when her aunt took Joyce and her sister to Chicago to attend a Cubs game. This was the first time

dress: remove the skin and feathers from an animal and cut it up for selling or cooking   **pinfeather**: a small feather just coming through the skin   **pliers**: a tool with two handles and jaws that you use to grip an object tightly   **thrill**: a strong feeling of excitement

NATIONAL BASEBALL HALL OF FAME LIBRARY

A Chicago Cubs baseball game in the 1920s. Many people liked watching the Cubs play.

Joyce had traveled outside Wisconsin. She loved the whole experience. Mostly she loved watching the baseball game.

When Joyce was 12 years old, she had an opportunity to play softball on her aunt's team. These players were 8 to 10 years older than Joyce. They let Joyce play because they said she was "almost as good as the older girls." She was the catcher. Since she had done so much **physical labor** on the farm, she was very strong and could hit and throw the ball far.

Joyce discovered she had natural ability, which meant that even without playing or practicing much, she was a very good player.

Aunt Esther's softball team in 1937, before Joyce joined it

physical labor: work using the body

4

"They Finally Got Tired of My Asking"

Joyce's country school was for children in first through eighth grades. In ninth grade, Joyce attended Lincoln Junior High School in Kenosha. Joyce remembers getting a new skirt and a maroon blouse to wear to school. She felt like she was really dressed up since she rarely had enough money to buy new clothes.

Joyce attended Kenosha High School for tenth through twelfth grades. There weren't school buses to take students to school during the 1940s. Joyce's father was working at Nash Motors again. So Joyce and her sisters had to get up early and ride with him to Kenosha.

Kenosha High School

In 1941, while Joyce was in high school, the United States began fighting in World War II. The United States Navy trained many of its sailors at the naval training station in Great Lakes, Illinois, 25 miles south of Kenosha.

Like the rest of the United States, **residents** of Kenosha tried to **support** people in the armed forces. Joyce's older sisters would invite the sailors to come to Kenosha during the weekend. The sisters and their friends would get a dance band to perform at one of the high schools. They'd provide snacks and have a big party.

The Great Lakes Training Center is still used today to train the United States Navy.

Sometimes one of Joyce's sisters invited sailors to stay overnight with the family. The sailors often didn't have enough money to stay in hotels. Some people in Kenosha thought it was wrong for girls to invite sailors to their home. But Joyce and her sisters felt this was a way they could help.

resident (**rez** uh duhnt): someone who lives in a certain place   support: help

19

While Joyce was in high school, she worked for her friend on his **truck farm**. She also **delivered** cabbages to a **sauerkraut** factory in Sturtevant, Wisconsin. Joyce was surprised to find German **prisoners of war** (POWs) working there. They were being kept as prisoners at the **POW camp** in Sturtevant. They worked at the sauerkraut plant during the day and returned to prison at night.

Prisoners of War in Wisconsin

During World War II, the United States and its **allies** fought battles all over the world. They captured many Japanese and German soldiers who fought against them. More than 400,000 of these prisoners of war were brought to the United States.

Why were prisoners brought thousands of miles to the United States? Because it would have been too difficult to guard them elsewhere. To take care of these prisoners outside the United States would have required building large prisons. The prisons might be attacked by enemy troops. Food, water, and other supplies would have to be shipped overseas to the prisons. Many soldiers would have to guard the prisoners instead of fighting enemy troops. It seemed wiser to bring the prisoners to the United States.

About 20,000 German and Japanese prisoners were sent to 39

truck farm: a small farm that grows many different vegetables   **delivered**: brought something to someone
sauerkraut (**sour** krout): pickled cabbage   **prisoner of war**: a person who is captured and held by an enemy during a war   **POW camp**: a camp where prisoners of war are kept, often just a collection of tents
ally: friend, especially during a war

20

POW camps in Wisconsin. Many of these camps were set up at county fairgrounds. Some were created by putting up thousands of tents surrounded by fences and guards. Camp Billy Mitchell, a POW camp in Milwaukee, was set up on the grounds of the Milwaukee County Airport.

Because many men from Wisconsin were now fighting in the war, there weren't enough workers to do jobs. So the prisoners were put to work. They were taken to factories and fields throughout Wisconsin to take the place of the missing workers.

A POW camp in Columbus, Wisconsin

After the war, the POWs were sent back to their home countries. Some of them later returned to Wisconsin to live.

German POWs marching to work from their camp

When Joyce was making deliveries, she would speak with the prisoners while she unloaded the cabbages from the truck. Many of the prisoners spoke English. Joyce said they acted nice and seemed just like many of the boys she knew in Kenosha. Some of the German prisoners even helped Joyce unload the truck.

When Joyce graduated from high school in 1943, she was 17 years old. She thought about going to college, but she was more interested in earning money. Like her father and 2 sisters, she wanted to work at Nash Motors. Although Nash Motors usually made cars, during World War II the factory made airplane engines for the United States Army.

Joyce when she was 18 years old

COURTESY OF JOYCE WESTERMAN

Joyce had to wait until she was 18 years old to work at Nash Motors. So for 6 months she helped her uncle on his farm. She also helped a cousin by milking his cows at night.

When Joyce turned 18, she filled out an application to work at Nash Motors. But she wasn't hired at first. Nash Motors had placed **advertisements** all over the country to get people to come to Kenosha to work for them. Nash Motors first hired people from outside Kenosha because they thought they could hire local people like Joyce any time.

Joyce didn't give up. She went to the **employment office** almost every day and asked if there was a job for her. Finally, she was hired. Joyce said, "They finally got tired of my asking."

Joyce was hired to work the night **shift**. She worked from about 4:00 p.m. until 12:30 a.m. and was paid $40 each week. Joyce thought this was a lot of money. She felt like she was now a grown-up since she was working at a job and making so much money.

advertisement (ad vur **tız** muhnt): a notice that a product or opportunity is offered or for sale   **employment office**: the part of a company that hires workers   **shift**: a period of work

But working nights created a problem for Joyce. Her father worked during the day, which meant she couldn't get a ride to work with him. She needed to have her own car to get to work. Her uncle helped her solve this problem.

When Joyce was offered the job at Nash Motors, her uncle asked her to continue to work on his farm instead of working at Nash Motors. Joyce told her uncle no. She explained that her father said that she shouldn't be doing so much heavy lifting. She could also earn more money working at Nash Motors. Even though he was **disappointed**, Joyce's uncle loaned her money to buy a car. He **appreciated** how much she had helped him on his farm.

Joyce with her first car, ready to drive to work

disappointed: let down or sad about something   **appreciated** (uh **pree** shee ay tid): enjoyed or valued

24

Joyce bought an old car for $345. Each week when she got paid, Joyce gave some money to her mother, saved a little bit for herself, and gave the rest to her uncle to repay the car loan. She paid him back as soon as she could.

Joyce's job was to help make airplane engines by **polishing** the **pistons**. Although she had never worked in a factory before, Joyce wasn't nervous. She was used to working with machinery. She had worked on cars with her dad. She knew how to change the oil and the **spark plugs** in a car. Joyce felt that she could do any kind of work that was put in front of her.

These women are working with pistons, just like Joyce did.

While Joyce was working at Nash Motors, she played on a softball team with other women who worked there. The softball team was her favorite part of working at Nash Motors. Later, that team experience gave her the opportunity to play professional baseball.

polishing: cleaning until something is shiny   piston: a tube-shaped piece of metal that moves up and down in an engine to produce energy   spark plug: the part of the engine that makes a spark to help burn the gasoline

Women at Work during World War II

World War II brought many opportunities for women. Millions of men joined the armed forces, so many jobs were left with no one to do them. For a long time, people believed that women were too weak to do jobs like working in factories. But during the war, women had to do these jobs. And they did them well, sometimes even better than men could do them.

WHI IMAGE ID 63367

This woman became a welder during the war. Being a welder is a difficult and dangerous job.

Women built ships, made airplanes and tanks, and did many other things that were needed to help fight the war. They also did jobs that had only been done by men, like delivering mail and driving buses and trucks. Women enjoyed working and earning money. By 1945, millions of women held jobs.

Most women wanted to continue working after the war ended.

But millions of men came back from the war, and they wanted their jobs back. Many women were asked to leave their jobs so that the returning **veterans** could work again. Some women agreed to quit and others were fired. But many fought to keep their jobs.

The effect of having so many women working during World War II was lasting. These women often had saved much of their wages since there was little to buy during the war. This money helped many families like Joyce's buy new homes and helped the economy grow during the 1950s.

WHI IMAGE ID 26350

These women are working in a factory making weapons for the war.

Women also had proven that they could do the same jobs as men. Today, women can work at any job thanks in part to those women who went to work during World War II.

veteran: someone who has served in the armed forces, especially during a war

5

Playing Ball during the War

On December 8, 1941, the United States **declared** war on Japan. This was the day after the Japanese navy attacked the United States at Pearl Harbor, Hawaii. Three days later, Japan's allies—Germany and Italy—declared war on the United States. World War II had begun.

In January 1942, President Roosevelt was asked if he thought men should still play professional baseball while the war was being fought. He wrote, "I honestly believe it would be best for the country to keep baseball going. . . . Everybody will work longer hours and harder than ever before. And that means they ought to have a chance for **recreation** and for taking their minds off their work even more than before."

declared: announced officially   **recreation** (rek ree **ay** shuhn): activities meant to be enjoyed, like sports and games

President Roosevelt declaring war on Germany

At the time, a man named P. K. **Wrigley** owned a chewing gum company. Wrigley wanted to help America win the war. His factories did many things to help. They sent free gum overseas to soldiers. They also stopped wrapping gum in **aluminum** foil, so that the aluminum could be used to make things needed for the war.

Wrigley was also the owner of the Chicago Cubs, a **major league baseball** team. He was worried about his baseball team. By the fall of 1942, more than half of the baseball players no longer played because they had joined the military. Wrigley worried that people would lose interest in baseball if no one played during the war.

Wrigley: rig lee   **aluminum**: uh **loo** muh nuhm   **Major League Baseball**: the top professional baseball league in the United States

29

Wrigley thought that if there weren't men to play baseball while the war was going on, why not have women play? After

the United States entered the war, many jobs that were only for men before were now open to women. Professional teams of women players could keep baseball alive during the war.

P. K. Wrigley wanted to help fight the war and keep baseball going.

During the 1930s, women's softball had been very popular all over the United States, particularly in Wrigley's hometown of Chicago. Since he knew women's ball had a big following, Wrigley decided to start a professional women's league.

In the spring of 1943, he helped form the All-American Girls Softball League. There were 4 teams that played during that first **season**: the South Bend Blue Sox (Indiana), the

season: the set of official games played in a year

30

Rockford Peaches (Illinois), the Racine Belles (Wisconsin), and the Kenosha Comets (Wisconsin). Over the next 12 years, several new teams were added, and some teams left the league.

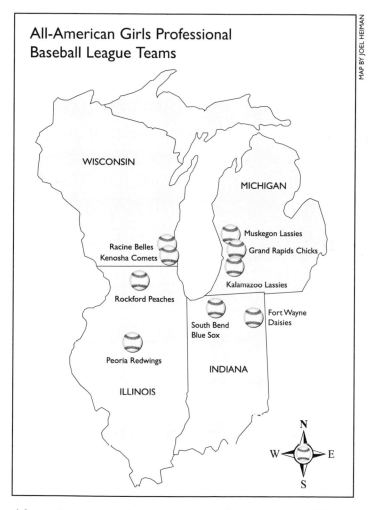

All-American Girls Professional
Baseball League Teams

MAP BY JOEL HEIMAN

WISCONSIN

MICHIGAN

Muskegon Lassies

Racine Belles
Kenosha Comets

Grand Rapids Chicks

Kalamazoo Lassies

Rockford Peaches

Fort Wayne
Daisies

South Bend
Blue Sox

Peoria Redwings

INDIANA

ILLINOIS

N
W ⦿ E
S

After a few years, there were many league teams. These
are the ones that lasted the longest.

What's in a Name?

In this book, we mostly use the name "All-American Girls Professional Baseball League" or "AAGPBL" because this is the name most people use. But the league went by other names too.

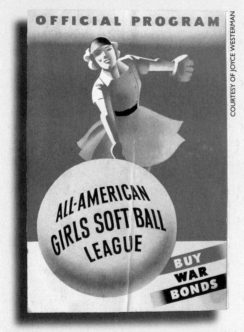

COURTESY OF JOYCE WESTERMAN

What year do you think this program might be from? What are your clues?

In 1943, the league was first called the All-American Girls Softball League. This name lasted until 1946, when it was changed to the All-American Girls Baseball League to show that they now played by the rules of men's Major League Baseball. In 1949 and 1950, the league was called the All-American Girls Professional Baseball League. From 1951 to 1954, the league was called the American Girls Baseball League.

All 4 of the original **host** cities had factories full of men and women who were busy building tanks and other weapons. Wrigley figured his women's league could help them relax after a hard day of work. Most games were played at night so workers could attend the games after work. The cities were all within 100 miles of Chicago. They were close enough together to let players travel on trains and later on buses to get to games.

Wrigley and his **advisers** had many decisions to make about the new league. What would be the rules of the game? Most women played softball instead of baseball. The league planners thought that men's baseball was faster and more exciting to watch.

They decided to create a game that included rules from both softball and baseball. They chose the 12-inch softball and underhand pitching commonly used in women's softball. But in the league, the pitcher stood 40 feet from home plate instead of 35 feet so that it would be easier to hit the ball.

host a person or place that provides services   **adviser**: a person who gives advice

The **base paths** were longer than in softball. Wrigley and his advisers hoped this would make for more **stolen bases**. It would be harder for the catcher to throw the ball all the way to the bases now that they were farther away.

They also used the men's base-running rules, which allowed runners to **lead off** and steal bases. Nine players were in the field instead of the 10 who played softball. All of these changes were done to make the game more exciting to watch.

Over the next 12 seasons, the rules changed almost every year. The ball got smaller. The distance between the bases got longer. The distance from the pitcher to home plate got longer. And the pitching styles changed from underhand to **sidearm**, and finally to the overhand pitching used in the men's league.

In the league's final 2 years (1953 and 1954), the women used the same size baseball as men. The distance from the pitcher's mound to home plate was the same as the men's.

base path: the area within which a base runner must stay when running between bases   **stolen base**: when a base runner is able to get from one base to the next during a pitch without the batter hitting the ball
lead off: when a base runner steps off a base before a pitch is thrown in order to be closer to the next base
sidearm: throwing with the arm going out to the side of the body rather than above or below the shoulder

But the length of the base paths was shorter than in men's baseball by 5 feet. The women proved that they could play the same game of baseball as men.

Wrigley also had to find good female baseball players. He hired 30 baseball **scouts** from the men's baseball league. They would look for outstanding softball players all over the United States and Canada. Hundreds of women were invited to try out for the league. Of these, only 280 were invited to the final tryouts in Chicago. Sixty of these women became the first women to ever play in their own professional baseball league.

scout: someone hired by a sports team to find new and better players

Women in the History of Baseball

When baseball was first played, people thought of it as a men's game. But pretty soon, women wanted to play ball too.

Women's colleges had baseball teams as early as 1866. In 1867, the first professional women's baseball team, called the Dolly Vardens, started in Philadelphia, Pennsylvania. They wore red dresses and played with a soft ball of yarn instead of a baseball.

Soon more women's teams began playing. In the 1880s and 1890s, women's teams traveled to different towns and played games against anyone who wanted to face them. They often played against local men's teams.

Women playing baseball was new and interesting, and many people watched the games.

A women's baseball team from around 1890

The players could often make good money by having people who wanted to watch pay for a ticket.

Not all teams played for money. Many women played on **amateur** teams. Teams formed in towns and at large factories, like the Nash Motors team Joyce played for.

amateur (**am** uh chur): doing something for fun and not for money

36

Before long, women got good enough at baseball to challenge the men. Travelling women's teams often beat teams of men. In 1898, Lizzie Arlington became the first woman to sign a **contract** to play baseball. Lizzie was a great pitcher. She was paid $100 a week to play baseball, which was a lot of money in 1898.

Another Lizzie—Lizzie Murphy—played for a team called the American League All Stars. In 1922, Lizzie and her team played against, and beat, the Boston Red Sox, a men's major league team. Lizzie played first base.

NATIONAL BASEBALL HALL OF FAME LIBRARY

Lizzie Murphy

In 1931, Jackie Mitchell struck out baseball greats Babe Ruth and Lou **Gehrig** in a game against the New York Yankees. After that happened, the major leagues banned contracts for women. No woman has played in an official major league baseball game since.

CHATTANOOGA HISTORY CENTER

Jackie Mitchell with Babe Ruth and Lou Gehrig

contract: an agreement between people or companies about what each will do for the other   **Gehrig**: ger ig

The league started its first season in 1943. They played 108 games during that first season. They played single games 6 days a week plus a **double header** on Sundays. Their only time off was when games were rained out.

Professional women's baseball offered something new and exciting. Wrigley expected that fans would come to the ballparks to see how well women could play what was considered a man's sport.

The league wanted to make sure fans would come back again and again. Wrigley thought it would help if the players looked **feminine**. He wanted the women to play like men but look like "ladies."

This meant several things. Both on and off the field, the players had to wear skirts in public. They could never smoke or drink in public either. They also had to have long hair, at least down to their shoulders.

double header: when the same two teams play two games against each other on the same day
feminine (fem uh nuhn): having to do with women and how they are supposed to look and act

Charm School

When the league was formed, P. K. Wrigley wanted to make sure the players looked "feminine" and behaved with good manners. To help them do this, he had players go to a special school for training in manners and **grooming**.

Before the season started, all of the players had to attend **charm school**. They received lessons in the "proper" ways of walking, sitting, speaking, choosing clothes, and applying makeup. They learned how to speak politely to gentlemen and how to walk across the room wearing high heels. And they learned how to cross their feet at the ankles when they were sitting. Many of the players thought this training was a waste of time, but others found it helpful.

When Joyce joined the league in 1945, players no longer had to attend charm school. But they still had to appear "feminine." Joyce later said, "You had to wear skirts all the time. You couldn't have short hair and you had to look nice, so I was always curling my hair. I'd play a ball game, come home, take a shower, and curl my hair for the next day so it would look nice. But I was a catcher, so it'd get messed up again."

The women in the league had to dress nicely and wear makeup.

grooming: the way you take care of your appearance or clothing   **charm school**: a school in which polite manners and proper behavior are taught

The players were even required to wear short skirts and lipstick when they played ball. Wrigley had a special baseball uniform made for the players. The uniform included a one-piece dress with tight shorts underneath and knee-high socks.

Many of the players hated wearing these uniforms. Pitchers had to pin their skirts down to avoid hitting them when they pitched the ball. Base runners collected many painful bruises and bloody skin from sliding with bare legs. But the players were tough. The bruises became a sign of **courage** among them.

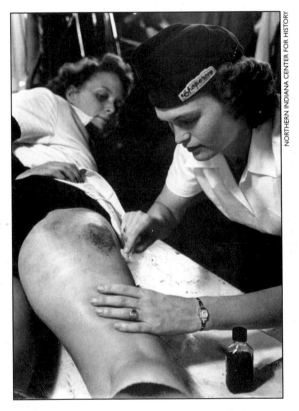

NORTHERN INDIANA CENTER FOR HISTORY

Bruises and scrapes were just part of the game.

courage: bravery or fearlessness

Bloomer Girls

When women began playing baseball in the 1860s, they were expected to wear clothing that covered most of their bodies. So they wore uniforms with long skirts, long sleeves, high necklines, and high-button shoes. These tight uniforms made **fielding** and batting difficult. Wasn't there something better for them to wear?

A few years earlier, in the late 1840s, Amelia Jenks Bloomer was one of many women who fought for women's rights, including the right to vote. In 1849, she began **publishing** her opinions in her own newspaper, *The Lily*.

A friend of hers began wearing loose pants like women wore in the country of Turkey. Bloomer liked how much freedom they gave her friend to move, so she began wearing the pants herself and **promoted** them in her newspaper.

Playing baseball in long skirts

Many women read about these pants that looked so comfortable. They began to wear them too. They called them "**bloomers**" because

fielding: catching and throwing the ball to try to get a player out in a baseball game   **publishing**: producing a book, magazine, newspaper, or any other printed material so that people can buy it   **promoted**: helped or encouraged to exist   **bloomers**: loose pants that gather at the knee and were popular with women in the late 1800s

Amelia Bloomer had made them popular.

So when female baseball players of the 1890s needed better uniforms that were easier to play in, they wore bloomers. Many people made fun of them for wearing these

Bloomers made it easier for women to play ball.

funny-looking uniforms. People started calling them Bloomer Girls. But the women loved playing baseball so much that they didn't listen to them.

Bloomers were out of style by the time the All-American Girls Professional Baseball League started. Joyce and her teammates wore one-piece dresses. Their uniforms didn't look as funny as bloomers, but they were much harder to play ball in.

Each team also had to hire a **chaperone**. This was an older woman whose job was to make sure the players followed the rules. She would also help them with any other problems they had.

Wrigley asked a lot of his players. In return, he offered an opportunity that American women had never dreamed possible. And he paid his players well to do something they loved to do: play ball!

chaperone (**shap** uh rohn): an adult or older person who looks after young people and makes sure they behave

6

Tryouts

About 6 months after she began working at Nash Motors, Joyce received a phone call asking her if she would be willing to help the Kenosha Comets. The Comets were one of the teams in the All-American Girls Softball League. Several players from the Comets had been **injured**. They needed more players.

Joyce had heard of the Comets, but she had never seen them play. She didn't know why they chose her to play for them. She thought perhaps someone from the Comets had heard about how well she played on her softball team at Nash Motors.

Joyce agreed to help the Comets. When she joined them, she was **amazed** by what she found. She'd never seen girls pitch the ball so fast before.

injured: hurt   amazed: surprised

Joyce was also surprised to see the players wearing skirts while they were playing ball. She thought, "I'm not going to wear those things. There's no way I would play ball in a skirt because coming from a farm you wore jeans. You had to wear skirts when you went to school, but we were not used to showing our legs like that. You'd be sliding in the dirt and your skirts would go up. That was a **no-no**."

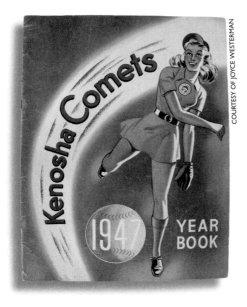

COURTESY OF JOYCE WESTERMAN

But after Joyce saw them play, she decided to wear the uniform even if she didn't like the idea. She wanted to play ball!

Joyce played with the Comets for one weekend. She played right field. When it was her turn to bat, she hit only one foul ball and struck out twice. She considered herself lucky to hit the ball at all because the pitches were so fast.

no-no: something not allowed

When the weekend ended, Joyce decided she wanted to continue to play baseball in the league. She thought, "If those girls can play professional ball, why can't I play too? If it's your dream to play ball and they're going to pay you to play ball, there wouldn't be any question in your mind. I gotta try out for this league. And I thought I was good enough to make it."

In the fall of 1944, tryouts for the league were held in Kenosha and Racine, Wisconsin. Thirty girls from all over Wisconsin attended the first 3-hour tryout camp in Kenosha. The following weekend, 50 girls attended the tryouts in Racine.

Joyce decided to try out for catcher. She thought that catching was the most important and difficult position to play. It would be hard for the league to find good catchers. She said, "I had caught a little bit when I was 12.... I thought, 'Boy if I'm going to get in this league, I think they'll need catchers. So I'll try out as a catcher.'"

Joyce played very well at the tryouts. She was one of 2 girls chosen to go to Chicago the following spring for the final tryouts. Joyce would now play against players who had been **recruited** from all over the United States. The best players in the tryouts would be chosen to play in the league.

Joyce didn't want to quit her job at Nash Motors since she didn't know if she would make the league. So before she went to Chicago, Joyce took a **leave of absence** from her job. This meant she could return to her job if she wasn't chosen to play.

When it was time for Joyce to go to Chicago in the spring of 1945, she was scared. She wasn't afraid of competing against other players. She was nervous about going to a big city. Joyce had rarely traveled outside Kenosha. Now she had to take a train to Chicago. Once she arrived, she had to find Wrigley Field, the place where the tryouts would take place. Joyce worried that she would get lost.

Joyce rode the train to Chicago without knowing what would happen when she arrived. She was 19 years old and scared. But someone from the league met Joyce at the train station when she arrived. He first took her to the Allerton

recruited (ri **kroo** tuhd): encouraged to join a group or organization   **leave of absence**: special time off from work

47

Hotel, where she would stay while she attended the tryouts. It was also the first time Joyce had ever stayed in a hotel.

At Wrigley Field, Joyce and the other girls had 2 weeks of tryouts. When Joyce returned home to Kenosha, she still didn't know if she had made the league. But soon she received a letter telling her that she had been chosen.

Joyce then quit her job at Nash Motors. She had been earning $40 a week working on airplane engines. Now she would be making $55 per week doing something she loved. Joyce was now a professional baseball player.

Joyce was nervous about going to Chicago.

7

"Am I Going to Be Able to Keep Up with These Girls?"

The United States had been involved in World War II for more than 3 years when Joyce joined the league. Throughout the war, the league tried to show its support for the soldiers. At the beginning of each game, one team would stand along the first base line from home plate. The other team would stand along the third base line. Together they formed the letter *V*, which stood for "**Victory**."

Supporting the soldiers with a V for Victory

victory: success in something

It was the league's way of reminding the fans to support the soldiers.

The league also tried to help the soldiers by providing them with entertainment. Joyce began her baseball **career** playing an **exhibition game** for soldiers who were training at Camp Ellis in Illinois. Then she joined her team, the Grand Rapids Chicks.

Joyce, in the middle, with some of her Grand Rapids teammates

career: a job   **exhibition** (eks uh **bish** uhn) **game**: a practice game that does not count for the season

Joyce was both nervous and excited when she joined the Chicks. Grand Rapids was one of the best teams in the league. Joyce was a **rookie** with little experience playing baseball compared to many of her teammates. She worried, "Am I going to be able to keep up with these girls?"

Joyce's manager made her even more nervous. When she joined the league, Joyce didn't know that many of the league's rules were different from the softball rules she was used to. In the league, runners could lead off the bases. The pitching distance to home plate was farther than when she'd played softball. The distance between the bases was longer too. This was all new to Joyce.

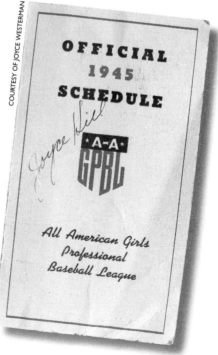

COURTESY OF JOYCE WESTERMAN

OFFICIAL 1945 SCHEDULE

A-A
GPBL

All American Girls Professional Baseball League

Joyce's manager would hold team meetings. He'd ask Joyce questions about the rules in front of the whole team. He knew she couldn't answer. Joyce felt embarrassed when she didn't know the rules.

rookie: someone in his or her first season with a sports team

51

Joyce was particularly nervous before games began. Her teammates tried to help her. They'd encourage her by saying things like, "Come on, Joyce, we know you can do it!"

Joyce became very quiet during her first year in the league. She only spoke when someone spoke to her first. She later said, "If I said 5 words to anybody, I did very well."

Joyce didn't want to fail, so she practiced extra hard. She did this during all 8 years she played in the league. Growing up on a farm, she already knew how to work hard. Now she wanted to work hard to become a better baseball player.

During that first year, Joyce practiced as much as she could. She spent a lot of time hitting, catching **fly balls**, catching balls pitched to her, and working on her throw to second base from home plate.

Joyce also carefully watched how the other girls played. She especially watched Dorothy "Mickey" **Maguire**, the Chicks' **starting** catcher. Mickey was one of the best catchers in the league. Joyce learned by studying what Mickey did as a catcher.

fly ball: a baseball hit high in the air   **Maguire**: muh **gwɪ** ur   **starting**: a player on a team, usually the best in a position, who plays at the start of the game, not sitting on the bench

Joyce and many of the other rookies spent most of the season **on the bench** watching their teammates play. But they still tried to help their team. They'd root for their teammates and cheer them on.

Mickey Maguire

Joyce only played in 9 of the 120 games the Grand Rapids Chicks played during the 1945 season. She batted 18 times and got 2 hits. It was hard for Joyce to watch most of the games instead of play. But she knew that she didn't have much experience and that Mickey Maguire was a better catcher.

on the bench: not playing in the game

Joyce loved being a player in the league. She liked hitting, and she liked catching too. Her hitting and fielding improved as the season wore on. She liked playing baseball more and more. The league must have liked her too. They asked her to play again the next season.

Viola "Tommie" Thompson, one of Joyce's teammates.

8

"I Was Just Too Serious about Everything"

Joyce began her second season playing for the South Bend Blue Sox. On May 1, 1946, she took a train to **Pascagoula**, Mississippi, where she reported for **spring training**. For 5 days, Joyce and all the other players in the league practiced and got in shape for the coming season.

COURTESY OF JOYCE WESTERMAN

Joyce in her South Bend uniform

In Pascagoula, they stayed in houses put up during the war for men who built navy ships. Joyce did not like sleeping there. There were **cockroaches** everywhere. The players slept with the

Pascagoula: pas kuh **goo** luh   **spring training**: a program of training and practice games to prepare baseball players for the season   **cockroach** (**kok** rohch): a brown or black insect that lives in warm, dark places and is a household pest

lights on because cockroaches don't come out in the light. When the girls walked around the city, they joked about the bugs. They made up funny names for the streets, like "Cockroach **Boulevard**."

When they left Pascagoula, the Blue Sox went on the road for a 2-week exhibition game tour. They played games in 5 states in the southern part of the United States.

One thing that surprised Joyce on this trip was seeing red soil. The soil in much of the southern United States is red. On the farm where Joyce grew up in Wisconsin, the soil was black. Joyce wondered how farmers could grow things in red soil.

Joyce was saddened by the **poverty** she saw. The poor **shacks** where many people lived reminded her of the broken-down home she grew up in after her family lost their home in Kenosha.

During her second season, Joyce was even more nervous that she wouldn't play well. She worried that she was going

boulevard (**bul** uh vahrd): a big city street, often with grass or trees in between the lanes
poverty: the state of being very poor   **shack**: a small, roughly built house or cabin

The South Bend Blue Sox in 1946. Joyce is the third from the left in the middle row.

to do something wrong and wouldn't get to stay in the league. She worked so hard and worried so much that she became ill.

The team sent Joyce to a doctor. He discovered that part of the reason why she was nervous was because she had low **blood sugar**. He gave her medicine that helped her, but Joyce continued to worry. She later said, "I was just too serious about everything. I just couldn't relax and play the game."

blood sugar: the amount of natural sugar present in your blood

Off the field, Joyce's second season was better than her first. She was less quiet, and she got to know her Blue Sox teammates better than the girls she'd played with in Grand Rapids.

Travel became easier and more fun during that second season too. The war was over. This meant that gas **rationing** was over. Each team in the league now had its own bus. The players didn't have to wait to catch trains or carry heavy suitcases from one train to another. Instead, they could load their suitcases underneath the bus and take them out when they arrived at the hotel where they would stay. This was very different from train travel, and the players loved it.

Players riding the bus to a game

rationing: limiting the amount of something that people are allowed to use

Riding on the buses was usually fun. The girls might sing or play cards. But it was tiring too. Well-**paved** highways hadn't been built yet. Cars and buses couldn't go as fast as they can today. Some of the bus rides would last many hours because it was hundreds of miles from one city to the next. Occasionally, they'd arrive just in time for their next game. The girls sometimes had to change into their uniforms right on the bus.

Joyce and her teammates often had a lot of free time between games. If they had a night game planned, they'd sleep late in the morning. They might go to a movie in the afternoon. They also did a lot of **window-shopping**. Joyce liked to buy clothes, but she and her teammates could window-shop all day without buying anything.

Joyce played more during her second season than during her first. She played in 21 games, batted 57 times, and got 7 hits. She also scored 6 runs, had 3 **runs batted in** (RBIs), and stole 7 bases. Although Joyce still didn't like wearing a skirt while she played, she was used to it and it no longer bothered her.

paved: covered with a hard material such as concrete or asphalt   **window-shopping**: looking at things in stores for fun without planning to buy them   **run batted in**: a run that is scored because of an action by the batter

During the last 2 weeks of the season, Joyce was sent to play for the Fort Wayne Daisies because they needed another player. Players could be loaned to other teams if an important player was hurt, sick, or unable to play.

COURTESY OF JOYCE WESTERMAN

WATCH JOYCE HILL PLAY BALL

One day soon after she joined the Daisies, Joyce was practicing throwing the ball to second base from her catcher's position behind home plate. One of her teammates, Faye Dancer, was told to stand at home plate and pretend to be the batter. She was told not to swing at the ball. Since Faye wasn't supposed to swing, it seemed safe for Joyce not to wear a **catcher's mask**. But Faye decided to take a slow, easy swing to make it look like a real game. When the pitcher threw the ball to home plate, Faye swung. The ball was tipped, and it hit Joyce right in the face. Joyce's nose was

catcher's mask: a padded metal mask that protects the catcher's face from the baseball and the bat

60

broken, and she wound up with 2 black eyes. Joyce knew this was an accident, and she and Faye eventually became good friends.

A few days later when Joyce began to play again, she broke her finger. Because of this, Joyce didn't play in any games during her 2 weeks on the Fort Wayne Daisies.

9

"There's No Crying in Baseball"

In 1946, the **Peoria** Redwings had the worst **record** in the league. One of the Redwings' problems was that their catchers did not play well. So before the 1947 season, the Redwings' manager looked for a new catcher. He decided that Joyce might be the solution to his team's poor catching problem. Joyce became the new starting catcher for the Peoria Redwings in 1947.

Before the season began, Joyce had her first opportunity to travel outside the United States. Spring training was held in the country of Cuba. In April 1947, Joyce and the other league players flew in a small airplane from Miami, Florida, to Havana, Cuba. During the flight, a storm rocked the plane. For many of the girls, including Joyce, this was their first time flying in an airplane. Many girls were afraid, but Joyce calmly looked out her window and enjoyed the storm.

Peoria: pee **or** ee uh   **record**: the number of wins and losses a team has

Joyce had many new and interesting experiences in Cuba, but she didn't like the food. They served powdered eggs and

Getting ready to fly to Cuba

alligator steaks. Joyce wouldn't try the alligator steak. But she did love the fresh pineapples she could buy from the street **vendors**.

Baseball was popular in Cuba, and the league games drew huge crowds. The Cubans were **impressed** that women could play ball so well.

The Redwings and their coach at a game in Cuba

vendor (**ven** dur): a person who sells something   **impressed**: surprised and respectful

Joyce played in 90 games during the 1947 season. Her **batting average** was .227. This was more than 100 points higher than she'd batted during the previous 2 seasons. Her catching also improved. Late in the season, the *Peoria Journal* reported:

Joyce has come a long way since she first **donned** the mask and pads in 1945. She has shown a strong arm and a sticky-fingered ability to hang on to the ball. There have been few if any **passed balls** called on her this year. Early in the season runners got the jump on her because she was slow in getting the ball away in a throw to the bag, but of late she has speeded up and runners are learning a great deal of **caution**.

When it comes to hitting she can hold her own with anyone on the club. A left-handed hitter, Hill hits the ball hard. In a game with **Muskegon** recently she pounded one against the right field fence on the fly, a **feat** that had not been accomplished at the stadium **previously**.

batting average: a measurement of how many times a batter makes a hit for every time he or she goes to bat; a perfect batting average is 1.000 ("one thousand"), which would mean the batter made a hit every time at bat **donned**: put on or wore **passed ball**: a ball thrown by the pitcher that the catcher should have caught but didn't, allowing a runner to get to the next base **caution** (**kaw** shun): care when doing something **Muskegon**: muh **skee** guhn **feat**: an act that shows great courage, strength, or skill **previously**: before

For her fourth year in the league in 1948, Joyce was happy to return to Peoria to play again for the Redwings. She was now playing more regularly, and she had developed close friendships with some of the girls on her team.

Joyce played well during the 1947 season. Here she is on the right after passing the ball to the pitcher, who is trying to tag out the runner.

Joyce and 3 other players rented a house together in Peoria. Joyce loved sharing this house with her teammates. But shortly after the season began, Joyce was traded to the Racine Belles. She was **heartbroken**. The 4 housemates had been **inseparable**. Joyce later said, "I cried. There's no crying in baseball, but I cried that time."

heartbroken: really sad   **inseparable**: impossible to break apart or separate

65

Joyce was one of the Redwings' leading hitters when she was traded. She was leading the team in **doubles**, **triples**, and runs batted in. But she had one major problem as a catcher. She had trouble throwing the ball to second base so that runners who were trying to steal would be tagged out.

Joyce later explained, "The thing that was hardest for me was throwing to second base. I had a good arm, but when  I was in Grand Rapids, I threw a little bit sidearm. They said catchers don't throw sidearm, and so they made me come up and throw like this [overhand]. When I did that, I lost a lot of time throwing to second base. I'd

Joyce, left, with a Peoria teammate in the house they rented

double: a base hit in which the batter reaches second base safely   **triple**: a base hit in which the batter reaches third base safely

66

tighten up and think, 'How in the world am I going to do this?' I got in the habit of bringing my arm up, **hesitating**, and then throwing. That cost me time with the runners running. I think if they would have left me alone, I'd have been much better."

COURTESY OF JOYCE WESTERMAN

Joyce was sad to leave Peoria. But she enjoyed playing in Racine too.

So Joyce was traded to the Belles for another catcher who was better at throwing out runners trying to steal bases. Joyce had bought a new car before the season began. She packed up her belongings and drove to join her new team.

Joyce was sad to leave her teammates, but she quickly learned to like being a Racine Belle. She developed many good friendships with her new teammates too. She also led the league in **defense** for all catchers that year.

hesitating: pausing before doing something   **defense**: stopping the other team from scoring

The Racine Belles, 1949. Joyce is second from the left in the back row.

Since Racine was near where Joyce's family lived in Pleasant Prairie, Joyce's mother sometimes invited the entire team to her home for dinner. She would cook a feast for Joyce's teammates. The girls had fun riding bikes, looking at the cows, and exploring the farm.

When the baseball season ended each year, Joyce had to find a job until she would begin playing again the following spring. These jobs were often hard to get because she would have to quit when the baseball season began. So she worked at many different jobs—whatever she could find. She cleaned rotten cabbage at a sauerkraut factory, sewed mattresses, and worked in the shipping room at a company that sold stockings and underwear.

Joyce returned to play for the Racine Belles in 1949. She had the worst experience of her career during that season. During a game, Joyce broke one of her fingers. A few days

later, the other catchers on her team were also hurt. The manager asked Joyce to catch one game even though she had a broken finger.

Playing ball could be dangerous. A chaperone takes care of Joyce's hurt ankle.

Joyce always wanted to help her team, so she agreed to play. Because her finger hurt so much, they taped 3 of her fingers together. Now she could barely close her hand to throw the ball. The other team quickly figured out that Joyce could barely throw the ball. They stole the most bases that had ever been stolen off of a catcher in league play. Even though this wasn't Joyce's fault because she was hurt, she still hates having this record.

10

Hitting the Ball Hard and Far

In 1950, Joyce returned to Peoria to play for the Redwings. She was brought in (along with another player) to improve their "weak catching department."

COURTESY OF JOYCE WESTERMAN

Joyce didn't play much during the first 2 months of the season. But everything changed for her in July when Mary Wisham, one of the Redwings' leading hitters, left the team because she was pregnant.

Leo Murphy, the team's manager, had to decide how to replace Mary Wisham and several other players who had been injured. He shifted some players into new positions and tried different **lineups**.

lineup (lin uhp): the players batting and fielding during a game

71

Joyce, left, and the Peoria Redwings

The Redwings' team bus.
Bus rides were often long,
but they could still be fun.

On July 14, he started Joyce in right field. She got 2 hits and scored a run. The Redwings won the game by the score of 8-3.

The next day, Joyce played right field again. She scored 2 runs and got a key hit to tie the game in the bottom of the eighth **inning**. The Redwings won the game in the ninth inning by a score of 5-4. The following day, Joyce pounded out another 3 hits and the Redwings won again.

inning: a part of a baseball game in which each team takes a turn batting; there are nine innings in a standard baseball game, plus extra innings if the teams are tied

Joyce remained the starting right fielder for the rest of the season. She finished the season with the best batting average on her team.

Why did Joyce suddenly hit so well? Perhaps it was because she wasn't playing catcher any more. She didn't have to worry about runners stealing second base. She had spent so much time worrying about stolen bases that it hurt her hitting. Now she became more comfortable. When she batted, she **consistently** hit the ball hard and far.

After the season ended, Joyce returned to Pleasant Prairie and married Ray Westerman. Ray had worked at Nash Motors too. He and Joyce met at a dance in Kenosha shortly after she began playing in the league. Ray became interested in Joyce partly because she was a baseball player.

COURTESY OF JOYCE WESTERMAN

Joyce and Ray

consistently: over and over again without change

73

When they were **engaged** to get married, Joyce told Ray they had to build their own house. She said she didn't want to lose their house like her parents had during the Depression. She wanted them to own their own home.

Ray agreed. They bought an acre of land from Joyce's uncle and a book on how to build a house. During the next 7 years, they worked on the house whenever they had free time and money to pay for the supplies they needed. They lived in that house for more than 30 years. Joyce proudly said, "We never owed a penny on our house."

Joyce continued to play in the league even after she got married. It was hard to be away from Ray for most of the summer, but Ray encouraged Joyce to play. He was proud

Joyce as a Peoria Redwing

engaged (en **gayjd**): agreed to marry someone

74

of her. She was also paid well to play
baseball. This helped them save money
for their house.

COURTESY OF JOYCE WESTERMAN

In 1951, Joyce played for Peoria
again. This year she played first base.
She was moved into the fourth spot
in the batting order. This was called
batting "cleanup." The cleanup hitter

A game ball Joyce kept from
the 1951 season

on most teams hits fourth in the batting
order. The cleanup hitter is considered the most powerful
hitter on the team and most likely to drive in runs (or "clean
up" the bases).

Joyce played 102 games in 1951, the most games she'd
play in any season in the league. She scored the most runs
in her career (51) and drove in the most runs (50). She
remained the cleanup hitter during her final season in 1952,
when she helped the South Bend Blue Sox win the league
championship.

11

Champions!

As the 1952 season approached, Joyce thought that it might be time to quit playing in the league. She had been married for more than a year and didn't want to be away from Ray anymore. She loved playing baseball, but the league had been having problems for several years.

Since the war had ended, more and more people were buying televisions. They now could watch men's baseball and other shows on TV without having to leave home. More people owned cars, which meant that they could go to movies and drive to restaurants for entertainment instead of attending league games. League teams began to have **financial** difficulties. Players were paid late and worried that they might not be paid at all. By the end of the 1954 season, these problems were so bad that the league **folded**.

financial (fuh **nan** shuhl): having to do with money   **folded**: failed or stopped operating

When Joyce received her contract in 1952 to play for the South Bend Blue Sox, she decided she wouldn't play. When she didn't report to spring training, the Blue Sox offered Joyce $100 a week to play. Joyce said she wasn't interested in playing, even though $100 a week was more money than she had ever been paid for playing in the league.

The Blue Sox badly wanted Joyce on their team. She was a powerful hitter and a good fielder at first base. The Blue Sox raised their offer to $110 a week. Joyce decided to play after all. She and Ray needed money so that they could pay for the materials to build their house. They could save most of the money Joyce earned from the Blue Sox to help them pay for their new house. And Joyce still loved playing ball.

Player Contracts

One of the reasons Joyce worried about remaining in the league was that she never knew from year to year whether she'd still be asked to play. In the spring, Joyce and the other players would find out whether they were invited back again when they received a letter in the mail with a contract. They'd find out in this letter if they would play on the same team again or on a different team. If they agreed to play, they could sign the one-year contract.

The contract meant that the player would play for the league instead of for one particular team. Until 1951, the league would recruit, train, and

The start of one of Joyce's league contracts

sign the players, then divide them so that every team would start the season evenly matched. After that, teams started to sign their own players.

In the early years, the league tried to create teams that were almost as good as each other to make the games more exciting to watch. This plan worked. More than 170,000 fans attended league games in 1943. In 1948, the league drew a record 910,000 fans.

During the 1952 season, Joyce hit .277, her highest batting average since she'd begun playing in the league. The Sox took second place during the **regular season**, but things did not look good for the **playoffs**.

About one week before the playoffs began, one of the Blue Sox players had an argument with the manager. He **suspended** her. Five other Blue Sox players quit the team because they thought it was unfair. Some of them were the best players on the team.

COURTESY OF JOYCE WESTERMAN

The South Bend Blue Sox in 1952. Joyce is third from the left in the back row.

regular season: the baseball games in a season before the playoffs   **playoffs**: a series of games between the best teams in a league to determine a champion   **suspended**: took someone off a team for a while

Before the next game, the Sox manager told the rest of the team that 6 players were no longer on the team. Everyone was stunned. Nobody moved or said a word. Finally, Joyce spoke. "We've got a ball game to play. Let's go play." It was as if a spell had been broken. The remaining 12 players went out on the field and played the game that day.

The South Bend Blue Sox began the playoffs playing against the Grand Rapids Chicks. The first team to win 2 of the 3 games would play in the championship **series**.

In the first game, the teams were tied 1–1 in the eighth inning. Joyce went up to bat and hit a **single**. Then she moved to second on a passed ball. When the next batter hit a **sacrifice bunt**, Joyce sprinted for third base. The Chicks' first baseman tried to throw Joyce out at third base. But the throw missed the third baseman, and Joyce ran for home. She scored the winning run, and the Blue Sox won 2–1.

Joyce's play at first base also helped her team win. In the ninth inning, the bases were loaded: Grand Rapids had a runner on every base with nobody out. The next hitter hit

series: a group of games played between the same two teams   **single**: a base hit in which the batter reaches first base safely   **sacrifice bunt**: when the batter holds the bat out and lets the ball hit it instead of swinging so the base runner can run to the next base even though the batter probably is out

a ground ball to Joyce at first base. Joyce threw it home for the **force out**. The next two batters **grounded out**, and the Blue Sox won the game.

Joyce sliding into third

In the next game, with her team leading 1–0 in the third inning, Joyce hit a **squeeze bunt** to drive in another run. Although she didn't bunt often, Joyce was an excellent bunter. She also scored her team's final run in the seventh inning. The Blue Sox won the second game by the score of 6–1.

Now the South Bend Blue Sox would play the Rockford Peaches for the league championship. The first team to win 3 games would be the champion.

force out: when a base runner must try to get to the next base because there are other base runners behind, but a fielder with the ball touches the base before the runner reaches it   **grounded out**: put out after the ball is hit along the ground, picked up by the fielding team, and used to put the runner out
squeeze bunt: when the batter bunts with a base runner on third and the runner charges toward home plate, trying to reach it before the catcher or another player can tag him or her out

Rockford won the first game by a score of 7–3. Joyce scored her team's second run in the losing cause.

South Bend won the next game in a 12-inning game by the score of 5–4. Joyce scored the winning run. She hit a single to open the inning. She advanced to third base after a **walk** and an out. Then she scored on a single. The series was now tied at 1–1.

In the third game, Joyce drove in her team's first run with a ground out in the fourth inning. But Rockford won the game by a score of 5–4 to take a 2–1 lead in the series.

South Bend evened the series in a 2–1, 10-inning victory the next day. Joyce drove in the winning run with a 2-out single with the bases loaded in the tenth inning. Joyce made 2 of her team's 8 hits in the game. The series was now tied 2–2. The winner of the next game would win the championship.

In the final game, Joyce drove in the first run of the game with a double. She also drove in another run in the seventh inning when she again successfully hit a squeeze bunt to score a run.

walk: when the batter goes to first base after the pitcher has thrown 4 pitches that don't go over home plate

South Bend won that championship game by the score of 6–3. The win was even sweeter because they'd played without the 6 players who had left the team. Joyce played a key role in every victory in the playoffs. For the first time in her 8 years in the league, Joyce played on the championship team. She later said, "It was unbelievable. I was so excited. . . . Everybody just pitched in. It was just **desire**. We showed people we could do it."

League champions!

desire: a strong wish or need for something or someone

12

A League of Their Own

When the 1952 season ended, Joyce decided she was finished playing in the league.

Each year Joyce had been gone from home most of the summer playing ball. After being married for 2 years, she didn't want to be away from Ray anymore.

It was hard for Joyce to quit because she loved playing, but she thought, "This can't go on forever. I think it's time that I hang it up and stay home and finish our house."

Joyce returned to Kenosha. She went back to work at Nash Motors, which was now called American Motors.

Since World War II had ended in 1945, women often were no longer welcome in the workplace. Many people believed women should be housewives again instead of working in factories. Even though the war had been over for many years when Joyce returned to American Motors, she was not welcome.

The company did many things to force Joyce and other women to quit their jobs. They gave them the hardest jobs to do. Many women quit because these jobs often were too hard. But Joyce knew that she could do any kind of work they put in front of her. When the company gave her the dirty job of **welding** fenders, she did it. When they gave her a heavy job putting motors on the **hoist**, she did it. Joyce thought, "They're not going to get rid of me that easy."

After Joyce stopped playing, she and Ray started a family.

welding: joining together two pieces of metal or plastic by heating them until they melt together   **hoist**: a piece of equipment used for lifting heavy objects

Joyce continued working at American Motors until after her first daughter, Janet, was born in 1955. Soon after Janet was born, Joyce returned to her job. She worked during the day, and Ray would work during the night. They continued building their house.

Working at American Motors, taking care of Janet, and working on the house made Joyce exhausted. One night she fell asleep standing up while she was giving Janet a bath. This scared Joyce so much that she quit her job. She didn't return to work until Janet and her younger sister, Judy, were old enough to go to school.

COURTESY OF JOYCE WESTERMAN

Joyce still has her Peoria Redwings uniform.

When Joyce returned to work, she got a job with the post office sorting mail and working as a mail clerk. She worked for the post office until she **retired** at the age of 62 in 1987.

One day in 1962, Joyce took out her old uniforms from the league. Janet and Judy had fun trying them on. They asked, "Mom, why don't you play for a team in Kenosha? Then we can watch you play."

Joyce thought this was a good idea. She joined a softball team and played for many years. When her daughters were older, Joyce played on the same teams with them. She also began coaching softball at Carthage College in Kenosha.

In 1988, Joyce and the players from the league received a special honor. The National Baseball Hall of Fame created a new exhibit called *Women in Baseball*. Joyce and 146 other players from the league attended the **ceremony**. They were honored for their accomplishments playing professional baseball.

retired: stopped working for good   **ceremony** (**ser** uh moh nee): a formal event to mark an important occasion

Four years later, a movie about the league was shown in theaters. It was called *A League of Their Own*. Several famous movie stars acted in it. Joyce and many other players from the league had small parts in the movie.

Joyce thought the movie was great. It also changed her life. After the movie was made, people who'd never heard of the league became very interested in it. Joyce was asked to give speeches about her life in the league. She often signs autographs after her speeches. Joyce says it makes her feel like a **celebrity**.

She said, "Kids really liked us and asked for autographs all the time, but I never saw myself as a big shot. Sometimes I couldn't understand why they're making such a big deal out of it. Even today, I think we get all this attention and all we were doing was playing ball and doing something we loved. I'd have done it for nothing probably. I think I'm just like anyone else. I didn't do anything special."

celebrity (suh **leb** ruh tee): a famous person

Title IX and the Courage of Women in Sports

Many new opportunities for women to play baseball and other sports have become available since the league ended in 1954. The passing of the **Title IX** law in 1972 has paved the way for millions of girls to play sports in high school and college.

In 1974, the rules of Little League Baseball were changed to permit girls to play. Since then, millions of girls have played Little League baseball and softball.

Joyce and the other women who played in the league didn't cause Title IX to be passed. But they did help to change the belief that women and girls are too weak and **delicate** to play sports like baseball. This helped open the door for the many opportunities to play sports that girls and women have today.

Title IX gave girls more opportunities to play sports.

Title IX (tı tuhl **nın**): a law that says people in schools cannot be treated differently whether they are male or female **delicate**: easily hurt

89

Many people would disagree with Joyce. They think she did do something special. When the All-American Girls Professional Baseball League was founded in 1943, women had few professional sports opportunities. There were professional female tennis players and golfers. But there were no team sports in which women were paid to play games against other women. The league changed this, and the women who played in the league showed that women had the talent and **determination** to play sports well.

Joyce in 2010

For the millions of fans who attended league games and the people who learned about the

determination: a strong desire to do something

league through the movie, Joyce and her fellow players did something very special. They were **pioneers** in women's sports. They showed that women could be great baseball players, and sometimes make their dreams come true. They were in a league of their own!

pioneer: one of the first people to do something

Appendix

Joyce's Time Line

1925 — Joyce Hill is born in Kenosha, Wisconsin, on December 29.

1931 — The Hills lose their home in Kenosha and move to Pleasant Prairie, Wisconsin.

Joyce plays her first game of catch with her uncle.

1935 — Joyce starts doing 4-H and gets her own calf to raise.

1936 — Joyce gets her first paying job at 10 years old, pulling weeds on a neighbor's farm for 10 cents an hour.

1937 — Joyce buys her bike for $5 with money she earns on her own.

1938 — Joyce joins her aunt's softball team and is almost as good as the other women, even though she is only 12.

1940 — Joyce starts going to Kenosha High School in Kenosha.

1941 — The United States enters World War II.

1943 — Joyce graduates from high school at age 17.

P. K. Wrigley starts the All-American Girls Softball League.

1944 — Joyce gets a job at Nash Motors. She buys a car for $345 with a loan from her uncle so she can drive to work.

Joyce joins a Nash Motors softball team and gets to play for the Kenosha Comets for one weekend.

1945 — Joyce tries out for the league at Wrigley Field in Chicago. She starts her first year in the league playing for the Grand Rapids Chicks.

1946 — Joyce plays for the South Bend Blue Sox. Spring training is held in Pascagoula, Mississippi.

1947 — Joyce plays for the Peoria Redwings. Joyce and other league players fly to Cuba for spring training.

1948 — Joyce starts the year with the Peoria Redwings but gets traded to the Racine Belles.

1949 — Joyce plays for the Racine Belles.

1950 — Joyce plays for the Peoria Redwings again and starts playing right field. Her batting improves now that she isn't the catcher, and she has the best batting average on her team.

Joyce marries Ray Westerman.

1951 — Joyce plays first base for the Peoria Redwings and bats cleanup.

1952 — Joyce plays for the South Bend Blue Sox. She has the best batting average of her career, and the Blue Sox win the league championship.

Joyce decides not to play again after the season ends.

1954 — The All-American Girls Professional Baseball League plays its last season.

1987 — Joyce retires from the post office.

1988 — The Baseball Hall of Fame honors Joyce and others with an exhibit called *Women in Baseball.*

1992 — The movie *A League of Their Own* comes out.

Glossary

Pronunciation Key

a   c<u>a</u>t (kat), pl<u>ai</u>d (plad),
h<u>a</u>lf (haf)

ah   f<u>a</u>ther (**fah** THur),
h<u>ea</u>rt (hahrt)

air   c<u>a</u>rry (**kair** ee), b<u>ear</u> (bair),
wh<u>ere</u> (whair)

aw   <u>a</u>ll (awl), l<u>aw</u> (law),
b<u>ou</u>ght (bawt)

ay   s<u>ay</u> (say), br<u>ea</u>k (brayk),
v<u>ei</u>n (vayn)

e   b<u>e</u>t (bet), s<u>ay</u>s (sez),
d<u>ea</u>f (def)

ee   b<u>ee</u> (bee), t<u>ea</u>m (teem),
f<u>ea</u>r (feer)

i   b<u>i</u>t (bit), w<u>o</u>men (**wim** uhn),
b<u>ui</u>ld (bild)

ı   <u>i</u>ce (ıs), l<u>ie</u> (lı), sk<u>y</u> (skı)

o   h<u>o</u>t (hot), w<u>a</u>tch (wotch)

oh   <u>o</u>pen (**oh** puhn), s<u>ew</u> (soh)

oi   b<u>oi</u>l (boil), b<u>oy</u> (boi)

oo   p<u>oo</u>l (pool), m<u>o</u>ve (moov),
sh<u>oe</u> (shoo)

or   <u>or</u>der (**or** dur), m<u>ore</u> (mor)

ou   h<u>ou</u>se (hous), n<u>ow</u> (nou)

u   g<u>oo</u>d (gud), sh<u>ou</u>ld (shud)

uh   c<u>u</u>p (kuhp), fl<u>oo</u>d (fluhd),
but<u>to</u>n (**buht** uhn)

ur   b<u>ur</u>n (burn), p<u>ear</u>l (purl),
b<u>ir</u>d (burd)

yoo   <u>u</u>se (yooz), f<u>ew</u> (fyoo),
v<u>iew</u> (vyoo)

hw   <u>wh</u>at (hwuht), <u>wh</u>en (hwen)

TH   <u>th</u>at (THat), brea<u>the</u> (breeTH)

zh   mea<u>s</u>ure (**mezh** ur),
gara<u>ge</u> (guh **razh**)

4-H: a club where kids learn about farming, healthy living, science, and other life skills

acre (**ay** kur): a measurement of area that is almost the size of a football field

advertisement (ad vur **tiz** muhnt): a notice that a product or opportunity is offered or for sale

adviser: a person who gives advice

ally: friend, especially during a war

amateur (**am** uh chur): doing something for fun and not for money

amazed: surprised

appreciated (uh **pree** shee ay tid): enjoyed or valued

award: an honor or present given to someone for doing something special

base path: the area within which a base runner must stay when running between bases

batting average: a measurement of how many times a batter makes a hit for every time he or she goes to bat; a perfect batting average is 1.000 ("one thousand"), which would mean the batter made a hit every time at bat

blood sugar: the amount of natural sugar present in your blood

bloomers: loose pants that gather at the knee and were popular with women in the late 1800s

boulevard (**bul** uh vahrd): a big city street, often with grass or trees in between the lanes

career: a job

catcher's mask: a padded metal mask that protects the catcher's face from the baseball and the bat

caution (**kaw** shun): care when doing something

celebrity (suh **leb** ruh tee): a famous person

ceremony (**ser** uh moh nee): a formal event to mark an important occasion

chaperone (**shap** uh rohn): an adult or older person who looks after young people and makes sure they behave

charm school: a school in which polite manners and proper behavior are taught

cockroach (**kok** rohch): a brown or black insect that lives in warm, dark places and is a household pest

consistently: over and over again without change

contract: an agreement between people or companies about what each will do for the other

courage: bravery or fearlessness

declared: announced officially

defense: stopping the other team from scoring

delicate: easily hurt

delivered: brought something to someone

desire: a strong wish or need for something or someone

determination: a strong desire to do something

disappointed: let down or sad about something

donned: put on or wore

double: a base hit in which the batter reaches second base safely

double header: when the same two teams play two games against each other on the same day

dress: remove the skin and feathers from an animal and cut it up for selling or cooking

economy (ee **kahn** uh mee): the amount of goods, services, and money that are made, bought, and sold by a group of people

embarrassed: feeling shy or uneasy about something

employment office: the part of a company that hires workers

engaged (en **gayjd**): agreed to marry someone

equipment (ee **kwip** muhnt): tools and machines needed or used for a particular purpose

exhibit (eg **zib** it): a public display of interesting things, often at a museum

exhibition (eks uh **bish** uhn) **game**: a practice game that does not count for the season

feat: an act that shows great courage, strength, or skill

feminine (**fem** uh nuhn): having to do with women and how they are supposed to look and act

fielding: catching and throwing the ball to try to get a player out in a baseball game

financial (fuh **nan** shuhl): having to do with money

fly ball: a baseball hit high in the air

folded: failed or stopped operating

force out: when a base runner must try to get to the next base because there are other base runners behind, but a fielder with the ball touches the base before the runner reaches it

Great Depression: the decade of the 1930s when many people in the United States had no jobs and were very poor

grooming: the way you take care of your appearance or clothing

grounded out: put out after the ball is hit along the ground, picked up by the fielding team, and used to tag or force a runner out

heartbroken: really sad

hesitating: pausing before doing something

hobo (**hoh** boh): a person who is poor and homeless, and often rides trains looking for work

hoist: a piece of equipment used for lifting heavy objects

homemaker: the member of a family who takes care of the home and children

host: a person or place that provides services

impressed: surprised and respectful

injured: hurt

inning: a part of a baseball game in which each team takes a turn batting; there are nine innings in a standard baseball game, plus extra innings if the teams are tied

inseparable: impossible to break apart or separate

laid off: sent home from a job without pay because there is not enough work to do

lead off: when a base runner steps off a base before a pitch is thrown in order to be closer to the next base

league (leeg): an organized group of sports clubs or teams

leave of absence: special time off from work

legally: in a way that is allowed by law

lime: a white powder used to keep barn floors dry and clean

line drive: a baseball hit fast and close to the ground rather than high in the air

lineup (lın uhp): the players batting and fielding during a game

Major League Baseball: the top professional baseball league in the United States

marbles: a children's game in which colorful glass balls are rolled along on the ground

mortgage (mor gij): money lent by a bank to buy a house

motor: engine

no-no: something not allowed

on the bench: not playing in the game

passed ball: a ball thrown by the pitcher that the catcher should have caught but didn't, allowing a runner to get to the next base

paved: covered with a hard material such as concrete or asphalt

physical labor: work using the body

pinfeather: a small feather just coming through the skin

pioneer: one of the first people to do something

piston: a tube-shaped piece of metal that moves up and down in an engine to produce energy

playoffs: a series of games between the best teams in a league to determine a champion

pliers: a tool with two handles and jaws that you use to grip an object tightly

polishing: cleaning until something is shiny

potbellied stove: a round iron stove that burns wood or coal and looks like a big belly

poverty: the state of being very poor

POW camp: a camp where prisoners of war are kept, often just a collection of tents

previously: before

prisoner of war: a person who is captured and held by an enemy during a war

professional (pruh **fesh** uh nul): someone who is paid to do something

promoted: helped or encouraged to exist

publishing: producing a book, magazine, newspaper, or any other printed material so that people can buy it

rationing: limiting the amount of something that people are allowed to use

record: the number of wins and losses a team has

recreation (rek ree **ay** shuhn): activities meant to be enjoyed, like sports and games

recruited (ri **kroo** tuhd): encouraged to join a group or organization

regular season: the baseball games in a season before the playoffs

resident (**rez** uh duhnt): someone who lives in a certain place

retired: stopped working for good

rookie: someone in his or her first season with a sports team

run batted in: a run that is scored because of an action by the batter

sacrifice bunt: when the batter holds the bat out and lets the ball hit it instead of swinging so the base runner can run to the next base even though the batter probably is out

sauerkraut (**sour** krout): pickled cabbage

scout: someone hired by a sports team to find new and better players

season: the set of official games played in a year

series: a group of games played between the same two teams

shack: a small, roughly built house or cabin

shift: a period of work

sidearm: throwing with the arm going out to the side of the body rather than above or below the shoulder

single: a base hit in which the batter reaches first base safely

spark plug: the part of the engine that makes a spark to help burn the gasoline

spring training: a program of training and practice games to prepare baseball players for the season

squeeze bunt: when the batter bunts with a base runner on third and the runner charges toward home plate, trying to reach it before the catcher or another player can tag him or her out

starting: a player on a team, usually the best in a position, who plays at the start of the game, not sitting on the bench

steer: a young male cow raised especially for its beef

stolen base: when a base runner is able to get from one base to the next during a pitch without the batter hitting the ball

support: help

suspended: took someone off a team for a while

thrill: a strong feeling of excitement

Title IX (**tī** tuhl **nīn**): a law that says people in schools cannot be treated differently whether they are male or female

triple: a base hit in which the batter reaches third base safely

truck farm: a small farm that grows many different vegetables

vendor (**ven** dur): a person who sells something

veteran: someone who has served in the armed forces, especially during a war

victory: success in something

walk: when the batter goes to first base after the pitcher has thrown 4 pitches that don't go over home plate

welding: joining together two pieces of metal or plastic by heating them until they melt together

window-shopping: looking at things in stores for fun without planning to buy them

World War I: conflict between the Allied Powers (France, Great Britain, Russia, and the United States) and the Central Powers (Germany, the Ottoman Empire, and Austria-Hungary) that lasted from 1914 to 1918

Reading Group Guide and Activities

Discussion Questions

- Why did Joyce feel embarrassed when she could play baseball better than boys? Is there anything you do really well, but that makes you feel embarrassed? Why do you feel that way?

- Joyce's father said, "You give a person 8 hours of work for 8 hours of pay. You do your very best. You don't just put in your time." So Joyce worked hard at everything she did. She practiced baseball all the time when she was in the league. And she did the hard jobs at Nash Motors. What do you work hard at? Why is it good to work hard?

- In the last few years of the league, the women's rules were almost the same as the rules for men's Major League Baseball. Why was it important that the women played by the same rules as the men? What did it mean to the league's players? Can you think of any games or sports where women and men still use different rules?

- How do you think Joyce felt after winning the league championship? Have you ever won something? What made it special?

- Joyce decided to stop playing baseball right after she had one of her best years and won the championship. Why did she decide to stop playing? What would you have done if you were her? Why?

Activities

❖ The Great Depression was a tough time for many people, and not only for Americans. If you have any relatives or family friends who were alive then, interview them to find out what life was like. Write questions before the interview, and take a video camera or tape recorder to document what is said. Write a report describing what you discover.

❖ There are many stories about how baseball was invented. Do research to learn about these stories. Who was involved? Where was baseball first played? What was the game like at first? Once you've done your research, decide which story you think is the truth. Make a class presentation showing reasons why each story of how baseball began might be true or not.

❖ Pretend you work for the National Baseball Hall of Fame. Your job is create ads for new exhibits. Come up with a poster that advertises the *Women in Baseball* exhibit about the All-American Girls Professional Baseball League. You can draw and color by hand or use a computer to make your poster. Think about what people will want to know about the exhibit. Make your poster exciting and interesting so people will want to come learn about the league.

To Learn More about Women in Baseball

Brill, Marlene Targ. *Winning Women in Baseball and Softball.* Hauppauge, NY: Barron's Educational Series, 2000.

Galt, Margot Fortunato. *Up to the Plate: The All American Girls Professional Baseball League.* Minneapolis: Lerner, 1995.

Green, Michelle Y., and Kadir Nelson (illustrator). *A Strong Right Arm: The Story of Mamie "Peanut" Johnson.* New York: Dial, 2002.

Macy, Sue. *A Whole New Ball Game: The Story of the All-American Girls Professional Baseball League.* New York: Puffin, 1993.

Rappaport, Doreen, Lyndall Callan, and Earl B. Lewis (illustrator). *Dirt on Their Skirts: The Story of the Young Women Who Won the World Championship.* New York: Dial, 2002.

Scott, Daisy. *The All-American Girls Professional Baseball League.* New York: McGraw-Hill School Division, 1994.

Acknowledgments

As a boy, baseball was my passion. I lived for Saturdays when I'd get to play Little League baseball, loved to play games of "wiffle ball" in the backyard with my brothers, and religiously read the box scores in the newspaper to track the progress of my beloved Chicago Cubs. Little did I know that nearly fifty years later I'd be able to revisit this passion and write a book about a professional baseball player. What a treat! As my childhood hero "Mr. Cub" Ernie Banks would say about his love for the game, "Let's play two!"

I am grateful to my friends, family members, and Wisconsin Historical Society staff for their invaluable suggestions and contributions to this book. Caroline Hoffman, Shayle Kann, Judy Landsman, and Deborah Waxman all helped to polish my language and enliven my stories. Caroline also worked with Joyce Westerman to provide many of the images in the book. Bobbie Malone, director of the Office of School Services, contributed her editorial skills and enthusiasm for this book. Andrew White, my editor at the Wisconsin Historical Society Press, offered his wisdom about baseball, history, writing, and selecting appropriate images to help shape this book. Thanks also to Mike Nemer at the press for his skilled production work.

Special thanks to Joyce Westerman for sharing the stories of your life with me. Your "can do" attitude is an inspiration to us all.

The following is a list of sources I consulted in writing this book:

Browne, Lois. *Girls of Summer: The Real Story of the All-American Girls Professional Baseball League*. Toronto: HarperCollins, 1992.

Fidler, Merrie A. *The Origins and History of the All-American Girls Professional Baseball League*. Jefferson, NC: McFarland and Company, 2006.

Galt, Margot Fortunato. *Up to the Plate: The All American Girls Professional Baseball League*. Minneapolis: Lerner, 1995.

Gregorich, Barbara. *Women at Play: The Story of Women in Baseball*. San Diego: Harcourt, Brace and Company, 1993.

Helmer, Diana Star. *Belles of the Ballpark*. Brookfield, CT: Millbrook, 1993.

Macy, Sue. *A Whole New Ball Game: The Story of the All-American Girls Professional Baseball League*. New York: Puffin, 1993.

Madden, W. C. *The Hoosiers of Summer*. Indianapolis: Guild Press, 1994.

———. *The Women of the All-American Girls Professional Baseball League: A Biographical Dictionary*. Jefferson, NC: McFarland and Company, 1997.

Index

This index points you to the pages where you can read about persons, places, and ideas. If you do not find the word you are looking for, try to think of another word that means about the same thing.

When you see a page number in **bold** it means there is a picture on that page.